2020
and me

Written and Illustrated by Sue Dower

Published in 2021 by Susan Dower
© Copyright Susan Dower

ISBN: 978-1-913898-25-0

Book & Cover Design by Russell Holden

Pixel Tweaks Publications
SELF PUBLISHING MADE SIMPLE

www.pixeltweakspublications.com

All illustrations © Copyright Susan Dower

A Catalogue record for this book is available from the British Library.

**The story of one person's journey through
a rather difficult year.**

The year 2020 was a bully,

It won't be easy to forget,

The stinging punches, that it threw at me,

I've not recovered yet...

CONTENTS

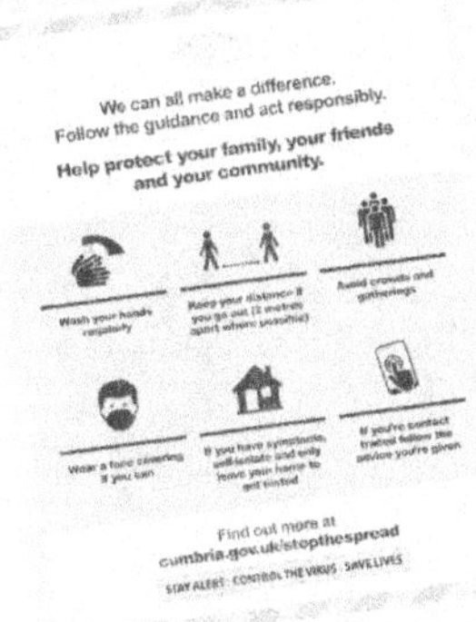

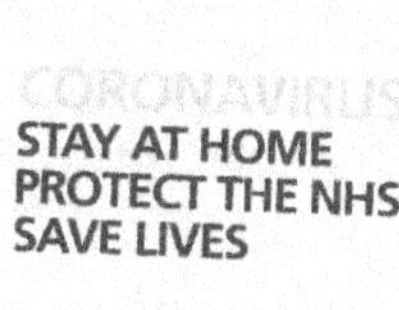

LOCKDOWN
15th March 2020

10 DOWNING STREET
LONDON SW1A 2AA

THE PRIME MINISTER

I am writing to you to update you on the steps we are taking to combat coronavirus.

In just a few short weeks, everyday life in this country has changed dramatically. We all feel the profound impact of coronavirus not just on ourselves, but on our loved ones and our communities.

I understand completely the difficulties this disruption has caused to your lives, businesses and jobs. But the action we have taken is absolutely necessary, for one very simple reason.

If too many people become seriously unwell at one time, the NHS will be unable to cope. This will cost lives. We must slow the spread of the disease, and reduce the number of people needing hospital treatment in order to save as many lives as possible.

That is why we are giving one simple instruction – you **must** stay at home.

You should not meet friends or relatives who do not live in your home. You may only leave your home for very limited purposes, such as buying food and medicine, exercising once a day and seeking medical attention. You can travel to and from work but should work from home if you can.

When you do have to leave your home, you should ensure, wherever possible, that you are two metres apart from anyone outside of your household.

These rules must be observed. So, if people break the rules, the police will issue fines and disperse gatherings.

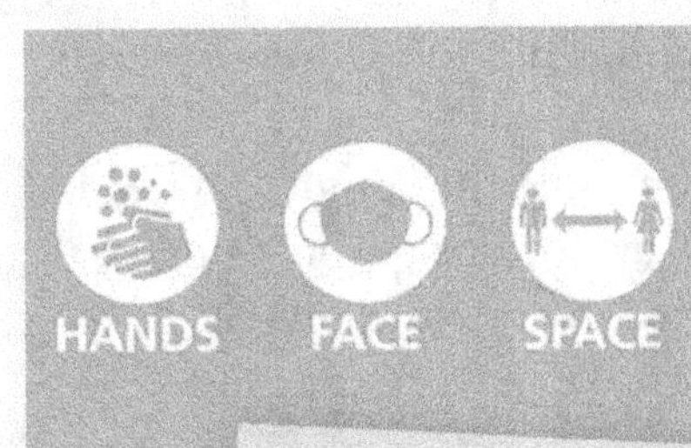

TWENTY DAYS

Isolation came on gradually,
I felt it coming near,
I felt it was inevitable,
Then suddenly, it was here.

I said goodbye to family,
I said goodbye to friends,
My sense of purpose disappeared,
I felt normality end.

It will be alright, I told myself.
There's plenty I can do,
I've got a list of DIY jobs,
And I could start decluttering too.

A flurry of activity followed,
with paintbrush, cloth and bleach,
I painted everything that was standing still
And was not too far out of reach.

Then came the cough and headache,
The symptoms of the 'thing'.
I tried to convince myself it wasn't,
But it had a worrying ring.

The daily art challenge kept me going,
The group chats with friends who cared.
I enjoyed their wit and banter,
And the funny videos we shared.

I worked on an old addiction,
And I discovered new ones too,
Have you watched Celebrity Catchphrase?
Well, I recommend strongly that you do…

Bargain Hunt's another gem,
I watched it every day.
Teams buy a load of rubbish,
And try to make it pay.

I cannot believe the things they buy,
Why would anyone want that dross!
Old chairs and buckets, chipped pots and plates,
Of course, they usually make a loss.
(Still, they're very cheerful about it.)

The headache is much better now.
The cough just comes and goes.
I'm exercising daily, am I healthier?
Heaven knows.

The sun keeps shining every day and I'm not listening to the news,
I'm trying to keep cheerful, and avoid the deadly blues.
I will survive, I know I will,
Life has thrown s*** at me before.
Can't say I'm a stronger person but I can surely take some more…

Isolation is quite a difficult game but I'm determined to compete.
I hope to play competitively and will try hard not to cheat.
I don't know how to approach this one, I haven't got a clue.
I can't draw on past experience because to me, it's very new.
I haven't got a game plan; I haven't got a coach,
But I know that moving forward is a very good approach.
A passive player who stands far back, will not go on to win.
So, I'll play up front, attack, attack, and take it on the chin.

I start the day with the crossword, one of my favourite things to do.
Sometimes it is a struggle, but I do complete a few.   (15-0)
I've started writing lately, which I used to do way back.
Like the crossword, it's a challenge, hope I haven't lost the knack.   (30-0)

I've also found, jigsaws on line, that's another little test.
I time myself to finish it and do better than my best.   (40-0)
I'm practising my drawing; I'm loving doing that.
I complete a daily challenge and post it on WhatsApp.   (GAME)

1-0

I communicate with friends on line and on the telephone too.
My family keep in touch as well, I'm so grateful that they do.   (15-0)

I spend hours working on my garden. It's looking good for this time of year.
It's had much more attention than it's ever had before.   (30-0)
I've also made friends with wild life that I didn't know was there.
A goldfinch in particular just lets me sit and stare.   (40-0)
My daily walk is such a treat, I've found a country lane.
I enjoy the views and the birdsong, despite it being solitary again.   (GAME)

2-0

Solitude, that's Isolation's big weapon in this game.
I can fight against it bravely but my defence is proving to be lame.   **(0-15)**
As time goes on, this tactic, seems to have more of a sting,
The lack of human contact is a very hurtful thing.   **(0-30)**

I like to think I'm self-sufficient, capable and strong,
but this opponent is trying to wear me down as the game becomes so long.   **(0-40)**
I've lost some independence, that really is a chore,
To rely on other people is something I've never done before. (I hate it)!   **(GAME)**

2-1

What's happened to my basic rights? Now there's lots that I can't do,
For example, meeting friends and family, is suddenly taboo.   **(0-15)**
I miss the physical contact, the freedom to just 'drop in',   **(0-30)**
Meeting someone accidentally, feels like a deadly sin.

I've lost my sense of purpose; I can't help others or do 'my bit'.
The problems are still there I know but I'm now far removed from it.   **(0-40)**
It used to matter what I said and did, now that's definitely not the case.
No one's listening to me now I know, because I cannot leave this place.   **(GAME)**

2-2

I feel that I don't matter, that I'm just wasting my precious time,
Merely trying to get through each day, without going, out of my mind.

Am I losing this game? What do you think?
I'll just refer you to the score.
Yes, the odds are stacked against me
But I'll keep coming back for more…

THIRTY-FIVE DAYS

This is beginning to annoy me now,
And that's a definite fact.
How many times will I be told?
No, you really can't do that…

I tried going to the beach today.
Is that too much to ask?
Couldn't get down the lane to park the car,
It's never been a difficult task.

Yellow signs instructed me,
No, you really can't park there.
Access is denied to you.
You'll have to go elsewhere.

So, I decided to try the Abbey,
Another special place,
But the yellow signs were there as well.
Rejection hit me in the face.

So, I chose a much more boring route.
I thought that would have to do.
At one point, I cut through the rugby fields,
Guess what?
KEEP OUT signs, had been put there too! (I don't believe it!)

I was feeling rather worthless, as it was, that's very true.
Now, dismissed and badly treated
And there's nothing I can do…

FORTY DAYS

Forty days in quarantine,
I want to scream and shout.
Forty days in quarantine,
And I'm wanting to get out.

People are still telling me,
That I'm very strong and tough,
But my inner voice is telling me,
That I've really had enough.

Yes, I have my daily challenges,
But I've had forty days of those,
Once, they gave me a sense of achievement,
And kept me on my toes.

But now, I really must admit,
That, that feeling is wearing thin,
The tasks seem quite repetitive,
And I don't care, lose or win.

The trouble is I hate routine,
And that's exactly what I've got.
So mundane, so bland, so easy
Purposeful?
It is not!

I need a sense of purpose,
I think I've mentioned that before,
I've lost it at the moment.
It's gone, and it's left a little sore.

Still, I'm sure I'll get it back again,
When my quarantine's at an end.
Until then, I'll be more positive
So, I don't go 'round the bend'.

I've had forty days in quarantine,
And I still want to scream and shout.
I'm still think of escaping,
But do not know how to get out…

FORTY-TWO DAYS

Forty-two days and counting,
And the last few, have been quite tough,
Because the rain has made its presence felt.
As if I haven't had enough.

Life is very restricted as it is,
And the bad weather is not great.
The jobs I want to do in the garden,
Are going to have to wait.

I need my daily exercise.
I need fresh air, to thrive.
I need, at times, to be out of the house,
If I'm going to survive.

Being housebound is no fun, I think.
I'm sure you will agree.
Do you know the term 'stir crazy'?
Well, that might apply to me.

Oops, I promised I'd be more positive,
I must try harder, I'm sure I can,
Because there is plenty to look forward to.
Yes, the government has a plan!

I'm told an announcement will soon be made,
Because things are looking good.
It seems we've passed the peak, right now.
Health experts said, one day we would.

I know I must be patient.
I know progress will be slow.
Restrictions will be lifted, gradually.
Quite right. That's the way to go…

FORTY-FOUR DAYS

I'm afraid I broke the rules today,
Is it such a sin?
My daughter invited me round to her back,
And I'm afraid that I went in.

I had no intention of doing it,
We are told to keep apart,
But she unlocked the garage, and I walked through,
And that was just the start…

A guilty feeling came over me,
But it didn't last too long,
Because my son-in-law kept telling me,
I was doing nothing wrong.

So, I relaxed and enjoyed the company.
The boys entertained me, as they do.
It was something I'd been missing.
Lately, times like this are few.

I had to leave eventually.
I had to drag myself away.
I went home to do my gardening.
There were jobs to do today.

When I did get back, with dad in charge,
The boys were already there.
They'd come prepared with axe and saws,
And energy to spare.

The tree stump was the issue,
I'd tried hard but it would not move.
With the pickaxe, they found it easy
And then they were really 'in the groove'.

What's next? What about the shrubbery?
A few feet off?
Do you think we should?
I nodded in agreement,
Wondering if they really could…

I didn't have time to worry,
They started at such a rate.
I can't criticise their attitude.
The enthusiasm, was just great.

My son-in-law was impressive.
He advised and showed the boys how.
They responded to the challenge,
And know how to do it now.

There were hairy moments, don't get me wrong,
Involving ladders, boughs and saw,
Resulting in a few blemishes,
That looked a little raw.

Twigs and leaves were flying everywhere,
Airborne branches were the norm,
The foliage was strewn around me,
Like the aftermath of a storm.

I surveyed the scene and wondered,
Where's all this debris going to go?
The tip is closed, we are in Lockdown,
As if I didn't know…

FORTY-SIX DAYS

I've been thinking for a while now,
Of exercising the car.
I've just wasted money insuring it,
Because I'm not allowed, to travel far.

So, it sits on the drive resplendent,
The sun glinting on the chrome,
It used to take me everywhere,
Now it never does leave home.

It used to be an asset,
It used to play a very big part,
But today when I turned the engine on,
It point blank, refused to start!

Damn!

I made a lot of phone calls,
But all to no avail.
Everywhere was closed, or couldn't help me
So, I suppose, I'm doomed to fail.

I thought I'd done with character building
But Lockdown is changing me, and how,
I never was accepting of my fate,
But I think I must be now…

FIFTY-ONE DAYS

My life might be changing, this weekend,
An announcement is going to be made.
Let's hope it will change for the better,
It's been difficult so far, I'm afraid.

I belong to a group known as the 'oldies'
Because of my age, I need to take extra care (apparently),
So, for protection, restrictions are greater.
I sometimes think it's a little unfair.

But that's how it is, and how it has been,
For fifty days now, or even more.
I'm hoping for good news on Sunday,
I deserve it I think, that's for sure.

There has been talk of extra precautions,
For people, like me, who have age.
An extension of Lockdown has been forecast,
The very thought of that fills me with rage.

So, Please Boris, don't discriminate against me.
Please treat me the same as the rest.
I'm one of nine million, remember,
Heaven help you, if we choose to protest.

I'm sure he will listen to reason.
We have supporters who tell him, don't fret,
The over seventies are sensible people.
They won't take risks with their safety, you bet.

It's true, I won't take any chances,
It's not worth it to break any rules,
I want to hang onto the time I've got left here.
Don't mistake me for one of the fools.

Let's hope it's an easing of measures,
It's something I'm longing to see,
This experience has changed me a little,
You might find me, a different me.

Life in Lockdown has taught me acceptance,
Of trying circumstances, I find myself in,
I'm not saying that it has been easy,
But deep down, I know, I can't win.

So, I've cried, moaned, complained and objected,
I've ranted, criticised, and imbibed,
I've made shopping lists and cleaned up the bird poo,
I think the seagulls need something prescribed!

Can you dose birds with Imodium?

Anyway, I'm putting all negativity behind me,
I'm moving on now and looking ahead,
Perhaps after Sunday, I'll feel a lot better,
I might find positivity instead…

FIFTY-THREE DAYS

I've got a problem at the moment,
And I'm somewhat at a loss,
As to know what to do about it,
You see I'm feeling very cross.

I'm alone and in isolation,
And the anger is like a curse,
I'm unable to vent my feelings,
So, it just festers, and gets much worse.

I feel so badly done to,
I feel resentment and the rest…
I feel a sense of great unfairness,
I need to get this off my chest.

There are questions that I need answering,
Of that there is no doubt,
You can call me irrational, (I'm sure that I am),
But I need to get it out.

Why can't I go to Tesco?
Why must I shop on line?
Why can't I ever get what I ask for?
Why are there substitutes all of the time?

Why all the fuss about V.E. day?
Why all the bunting, street parties and cake?
Do I want to pretend that I'm jolly?
No, I do not, for goodness sake!

Why can't I go to the tip when I want to?
And dispose of the debris I've got,
It's like the day of the Triffids in my garage,
Am I supposed to let it just rot?

Why do my portraits not look like they should do?
Why can't I get a likeness? I usually can,
Why can't I give up and admit I am failing?
Why is none of it going to plan?

Why can't I complete my latest crossword?
Twenty-seven thousand six hundred and three.
Why can't I fathom out the clues like I usually do?
Why do they make no sense to me?

Why do I have sciatica at this moment in time?
I've never had it before.
Why don't the tablets stop it from hurting?
What other aches and pains are in store?

I know all these issues are trivial,
Even so they are causing me grief,
I can't wait to get out of isolation,
I urgently need some relief.

FIFTY-FIVE DAYS

That's another day gone whilst in Lockdown,
Another day I can't afford to lose,
Another day when I've achieved nothing at all,
Another day when I can't choose.

Another day when my diary is clear,
Another day when I'm totally free,
Another day with no appointments to keep,
Another day becoming a different me…

FIFTY-EIGHT DAYS

The Prime Minister spoke to the nation today,
I was hoping to hear something good.
I was hoping he might ease restrictions for us,
I really did think that he would.

Things looked promising at the beginning,
I sat waiting, and hoped for the best,
He was measured and sombre in his delivery,
Then he told us we'd not passed the test.

His plan looked quite clear,
There was a scale one to five,
With five being the worst place to be,
We had started the descent and were slowly going down,
But we hadn't yet reached number three.

Three and a half was the place we found ourselves in,
We still had a long way to go,
He said we were definitely making good progress,
But going back to normal, would be quite slow.

I felt deflated and worried as to what was to come,
But I still had a vestige of hope,
He talked briefly about the effect continued lockdown might have,
On our mental state, and if we could cope.

Here comes the good news I thought, but oh no,
Of that, there was no more talk.
The next thing he said was people must go to work,
Avoid public transport, use their bicycle, or walk.

Then he said we are allowed to go to the park,
Sit in the sunshine and enjoy the view.
I'm sorry, but haven't we always been able to do that?
Does he think this is something quite new?

It all became very confusing after that,
And I'm really not sure I understood,
What we can, or what we cannot do,
I'm wondering now if this plan is so good.

"Stay alert" was the only new message I got from it,
As far as I can see, things are, just the same.
What does 'stay alert' mean anyway, I really don't know,
It's just jargon, to give it a name.

Come on Boris!
I need you to be far more definite,
I need you to be far more clear,
I need you to improve as a communicator,
You are quite hopeless in that role, I fear…

FIFTY-NINE DAYS

I went out for a drive in the car, earlier on,
I don't want the battery flattened again,
Added to the fact at the moment, I can't walk very far,
Thanks to the sciatica, which is giving me pain.

I'm pleased to say, I saw signs of normality,
On my journey to Walney and back,
K.F.C. drive through and the golf course were open,
Perhaps, after all, we are on the right track.

The recycling centre was in full swing too,
Long queues in the road made that clear,
I'll just wait for the rush to subside a bit more,
Then I'll be visiting myself, have no fear.

The Prime Minister's speech hadn't given me much hope,
Of them easing restrictions, and helping us out,
But his minister announced a few measures the next day,
Which would improve things for some, there's no doubt.

We're allowed to go further afield in the car,
We're allowed to exercise more often each day,
We're allowed to meet one of our friends in a big open space,
And play sport with another person, they say.

Garden centres will open on Wednesday, I am told,
That's good news for me, because, as you know
My garden is important, especially now,
It gives me pleasure to watch my plants grow.

For the moment, I have to be happy with that,
A slight improvement but not really enough,
So as usual I will keep on just 'hanging on in',
Hoping for the rules to become a little less tough…

SIXTY-FIVE DAYS

It doesn't take much to upset me right now,
My feelings have become a little bit raw,
The slightest thing is enough to annoy me
And, I'm quite capable of going too far.

There was an incident this morning, whilst out walking,
I had road rage, is that really like me?
I was 'cut up' by a newly-born cyclist,
With no idea or sense, of where she should be.

She said 'sorry' but that did not assuage me,
I was cross, I had anger to spare,
I was inches from being rammed into,
She rode off, looking back with a glare.

I met her again a few minutes later,
I was crossing a field and she was there,
I'm afraid I pointed my finger and remonstrated,
I expected abuse, but was too cross to care.

I told her of her misdemeanours,
Of how she was too close and overtaking on the inside,
She accepted she was wrong and apologised,
I felt my anger begin to subside.

It will happen again though, and I know it,
There are lots of new cyclists on the road,
In Lockdown people have taken up this hobby,
But for my sake please, read the Highway Code!

SIXTY-SEVEN DAYS

It seems we're moving into a new phase now,
On our way down to number three.
A new phase called Acceptance,
A case of 'live with it' and see.

At the beginning we were told to fight against it,
That we were in a state of war,
That we should use tactics to defeat it,
That we would triumph without a scar.

The plan was to eradicate,
The message was quite clear,
We'd hit it every way we could,
It would surrender and then disappear.

The message is quite different now,
It's more conciliatory, have we given in?
Have we realised we're not winning?
Must we just 'take it on the chin'?

We are battle-worn and weary,
We are Lockdown crazy, nearly mad,
Perhaps we should now, just embrace it,
Perhaps that wouldn't be too bad.

This virus isn't going anywhere,
It's determined not to leave,
So, I suppose we'll learn to manage it,
And keep a vaccine up our sleeve…

SEVENTY DAYS

A few weeks ago, Barrow was called a hot spot,
With more cases of Covid than all of the rest.
We were right at the top of the statistics,
You could say, we were not at our best.

Of course, the papers made it their top story,
We became quite famous, almost overnight,
As 'One of the remotest towns' in the country,
How could this happen? It didn't seem right.

But it was true, they had the figures to prove it,
We'd not been successful in stopping the spread,
Excuses were made, but the fact is, we'd done badly,
All we could do now, was try harder instead.

So, despite the so-called deprivation and terraced housing,
Despite the industrial illness, diabetes and the rest,
Despite the high blood pressure, obesity and asthma,
As the weeks go by, we are passing the test.

Life at the hospital is returning to normal,
With only one Covid patient in Intensive Care,
And only two more to be found on the general wards,
Looks like, after all, we are getting somewhere.

It would be interesting to now compare our progress,
With other towns, who are in the same boat,
To see if we still top the table,
Or if we are able to let ourselves gloat…

SEVENTY-ONE DAYS

It's Bank Holiday, Saturday morning,
I'm frustrated and ready to pop,
All I want is a few bags of top soil,
But, of course, I mustn't go to the shop.

So, I'll buy it on line, it'll be easy,
Click and collect or delivery will be okay,
But, 'I'm afraid this product doesn't qualify for that',
Everywhere I try, that is all they will say.

So, I'll break the rules and go shopping in person,
'Will someone help me and put the bags in the car'?
'No, I'm sorry, we must keep our distance',
That suggestion didn't get me very far.

So, I'll try one of our local garden centres,
I'm sure they will add me to their rounds,
Yes, they have top soil and they will deliver it,
But it comes loose and will cost sixty pounds!

So, I'll try Amazon, because I just trust them,
They'll have top soil and will deliver it for free,
But, just a moment, sixteen pounds for one bag now,
That's four times the price it should be!!

I can't believe such a level of exploitation,
On principle, I will not let them win,
I will suffer and manage without it,
No wonder my patience is wearing so thin…

SEVENTY-TWO DAYS

There's a scandal in Parliament at the moment,
It seems Dominic Cummings has broken a rule,
He left London and went up to Durham,
At the peak of the Pandemic,
(What?)
Is he a fool!

The Government said that we must not travel,
We must stay at home and not go too far,
But he ignored this safety instruction,
And travelled two hundred and sixty miles in his car.

He is the Prime Minister's most senior advisor,
Part of the committee, who were giving the advice.
He went up north to see his extended family,
Not only that, it seems, he made the trip twice!

How arrogant, irresponsible and disdainful,
Does he really think he doesn't need to obey?
Whilst we make sacrifices and do his bidding,
And he has it all his own way.

Eight weeks have gone by since this happened,
It's taken that long for the news to come out,
During this time the Government has said nothing.
A political cover up, again, there's no doubt!

Of course, there are calls now for his resignation,
Recently, two ministers have resigned for much less.
But up until now, he has the backing of his colleagues.
What happens next, we can only just guess…

SEVENTY-THREE DAYS

I've just had a realisation,
Lockdown has made me a different me,
I'm suddenly pathetic and dependent,
And I don't like what I see.

And, if that isn't bad enough,
There are other traits there too,
Like, being demanding and resentful,
I'm afraid that it's all true.

So, today is the day it all changes,
I know what I'm going to do.
I'm going to go out and about more often,
And find a social-distancing queue!...

SEVENTY-FOUR DAYS

Dominic Cummings has just made a statement,
I was thinking he probably would,
He said he wanted to justify his recent behaviour,
And explain that his intentions were good.

He said he didn't regret his decisions,
Exceptional circumstances were quite evident just then,
And that he was balancing the safety of his family,
With the extreme situation at Number Ten.

Now, I know he's a very important person,
Playing a vital and important part,
But the fact is two rules have been broken,
Which he helped put in place at the start.

He drove to Durham in his car when we were not to,
He didn't isolate himself when he got there,
He went outside when unwell and infected,
What about others? Did he not care?

In my opinion, his behaviour is disgraceful,
He has treated us all with contempt,
Does he think because he's clever and in high places,
That he's the one person who should be exempt?

Of course, the Prime Minister has given him his backing,
Saying he behaved responsibly, so won't take him to task,
Also, that 'reasonable people' wouldn't condemn him,
What does that say about me, might I ask?...

SEVENTY-SEVEN DAYS

I broke my curfew today and went shopping,
Because I'm telling you, I've just had enough,
Of being dependent on other people,
And not being able to choose my own stuff.

I've had eleven weeks, now, stuck in quarantine,
I've spent hours making shopping lists galore,
I've been supplied with what I have needed,
But I haven't been anywhere near a store.

So today I had made my mind up,
And, armed with some hand wipes, and a surgical mask,
I set off with a degree of apprehension,
Determined to complete this usually ordinary task.

I went at a time, which was reserved for us 'oldies',
And, it was quiet, I have to admit,
Hand sanitiser was there, at the entrance,
So, I obviously, made good use of it.

I took a trolley, and used a hand wipe,
And I walked in through the open door,
A one-way system was clearly marked out for me,
I had to follow the arrows on the floor.

I managed to do it, without much fuss,
I am really delighted to say,
Only once, when not paying attention,
Was I informed; I was going the wrong way.

I bought most of the things that I wanted,
Some stock was missing, of that there's no doubt,
But I think I'll take the risk again, next week,
Despite feeling guilty, it was good to be out.

Grayson Perry is an artist
Who is reasonably well known,
But I've got to know him better
And my respect for him has grown.

During Lockdown, he's been appearing,
Every week on the T.V.,
He is hosting an art club programme,
Which is really interesting me.

He's very casual in his appearance,
And he doesn't seem to care,
But there are hidden depths to this man,
He has an alter ego, known as Claire.

However, he's appearing as himself,
And he concentrates on the art,
He is passionate about it,
Explaining, it can play a very big part.

Especially at this time of Lockdown,
When, lacking structure and full of doubt,
We can be creative and express ourselves,
And let our feelings out.

He shows how art can lift our mood,
And give us a warm glow,
He asks people with artistic talents,
To complete a piece of artwork on the show.

He invites members of the public,
And a few 'celebrities' too,
To submit examples of their paintings,
So, he can give them a review.

He selects some of his favourites,
And there's delight when they hear him say,
'I'm putting it in my exhibition',
It really makes their day.

This is when he's always at his best,
Conversing, via video, I find,
When he's talking to amateur artists,
About their work and the reasons behind.

He is so warm and understanding,
He can listen and advise,
He can encourage and find the positives,
He can reassure and sympathise.

He explains his theories clearly,
He makes it plain so I can see.
Not pompous, or patronising,
But just ordinary, as it should be.

I shall miss him when Lockdown is over,
To my mind, he is really, a star,
I hope to visit his exhibition, if I can do,
Will they allow me to travel that far?...

EIGHTY-FOUR DAYS

It's been a torrid two months for the Government,
I really have to say.
First of all, the Prime Minister was virus-ridden,
And could not lead the way.

Then, other colleagues followed,
As if that wasn't enough,
Our infection rate just rocketed,
And things became quite tough.

As we topped the European figures,
The answer had to be,
Stringent measures and a lockdown,
Perhaps too late, we'd have to see.

We were told to test and test and test,
And do it with some speed,
But some of the tests were unreliable,
And the results were difficult to read.

After a while when testing improved somewhat,
A track and trace plan was worked out,
But that foundered and did not work at all,
Another blow, no doubt!

But there was worse to follow,
Mr Cummings' bad behaviour came to light,
The Prime Minister did not dismiss him,
Instead, backed him; that's not right! (surely?)

A senior aide had shown blatant disrespect,
And was not made to pay.
There was widespread disapproval,
Dissent, you could even say,

So now there's been a massive shake up,
The Prime Minister has taken back control,
Two new committees have been formed,
And Dominic will play a lesser role.

Yet another victim of The Virus,
It will go unrecorded that's for sure,
But just like all the others,
A case for which there was no cure.

A loving relationship at the beginning,
But Lockdown gradually rubbed it out,
Forced apart for shielding reasons,
Meant uncertainties and doubt.

Reassurance was what was needed,
But it wasn't always there,
So, the anxiety took over,
And it became too much to bear.

Circumstances caused this break up,
It really is a shame,
But in this abnormal situation,
I know where to lay the blame…

NINETY-FOUR DAYS

My son just asked what I've been doing,
As a joke I had to say,
I've been drinking Prosecco and complaining,
Hoping better times are on the way.

Restrictions have been eased somewhat,
Single people have had good news,
Those like me can form a 'social bubble',
With one other household, and I can choose.

I'm already seeing friends in our gardens,
Meeting regularly, face to face,
In rotten weather, I use the open garage,
It serves well as a meeting place.

But now, I can actually go inside,
Someone else's house. Yes, that's OK,
I could even take my pyjamas,
And have an overnight stay!
(What?)

Non-essential shops opened up this morning,
The government is encouraging us to spend,
People didn't need twice telling,
The lack of retail therapy, at an end.

Sport deprivation has also been a problem,
For many people, including me,
But football matches have resumed this week,
Other sports will follow, hopefully.

Restaurants and pubs are wanting to open,
But that's easier said than done,
Because the two-metre rule is still in place,
It needs reducing, perhaps to one.

My holiday has been cancelled,
The live tennis in London might have to wait,
My social life is virtually non-existent,
Oh my, I'm still in quite a sorry state...

ONE HUNDRED AND FIVE DAYS

An audible cheer went up in parliament,
When the Prime Minister made the vow,
That the pubs would be allowed to open,
In a couple of weeks from now.

The fourth of July is when it's happening,
Hairdressers, cinemas and restaurants too,
And we'll be able to stand a little closer,
In our social-distancing queue.

But, suddenly, mass migrations to the beaches,
Bodies crammed together on the sand,
A virus-friendly situation,
This was not what had been planned.

Why can't they be sensible and patient?
It's only a short time now to go,
Before restrictions are relaxed even further,
And there'll be improvements, I just know.

ONE HUNDRED AND FORTY-FIVE DAYS

Life is slowly becoming more bearable,
As restrictions continue to ease,
But, I'm afraid, it still is nowhere near normal
And I still am not easy to please.

I am impatient, intolerant, frustrated,
Disbelieving, and often, confused,
It's a struggle to keep my composure,
I feel battered and somewhat abused.

On the bright side, I have had a haircut,
I've had my tea at our pub, the Bay Horse,
I've had the long-awaited broken tooth extraction,
So, I should feel much better, of course.

I went for Covid training at the Women's Centre on Monday,
New safety measures were discussed and were put to the test.
I was invited to return to my volunteering duties,
A date, later in August, they said, would be best.

The Centre continues to provide a much-needed service,
Throughout Lockdown, referrals are high,
Extreme circumstances, are exacerbating the problems,
Women are facing and I can understand why.

I have received the dreaded email,
I expected it, I must say,
I can't go to London to see the tennis,
No fans allowed to watch the play.

So, no trips for the foreseeable future,
The highlight of the month has had to be,
A drive down the A590,
As far as Milnthorpe, oh dear me!

Suddenly, I've realised there's a sadness,
I didn't have a clue,
That it's been gnawing at the edge of me,
And now is slowly seeping through.

It's dampening the anger and defiance,
And the will I have to win,
It's making me tearful and reflective,
About the state that I am in.

TWO-HUNDRED AND TEN DAYS

You might think that I am demented,
You are entitled to think what you like.
But I am definitely feeling much brighter,
Since I discovered Mr Cormoran Strike.

He is a detective in a series of novels,
He is invented, he's not even real,
But the writer's clever insight and detail,
Bring him alive for me; astounding, I feel.

Crime fiction never was my favourite genre,
I read P.D James for a while, a long time ago,
But, now, I'm wallowing in blood, guts and tragedy,
Just to see how he copes with it all, (yes, I know!) …

It's irrational, but it's like an addiction,
Five thirty a.m. and I'm in Denmark Street,
Admiring how he deals with a psychotic client,
Taking the case, despite the dangers he'll meet.

I wouldn't mind, but it's not the first time I've read it,
I know exactly what the outcome is, but even so,
I want to relive it all as it happens,
A cause for concern, you might say, (yes, I know) …

TWO HUNDRED AND TWENTY-SEVEN DAYS

They always said that there was worse to come,
We've been battered and it has been hard,
But the threatened second wave has hit us early,
And has caught us off our guard.

Now, I feel like I am floundering,
Like I'm swimming aimlessly around,
Wading through tiers one, two, three and curfews,
Trying to find some solid ground.

It doesn't seem to matter which way I decide to turn,
I want to put my feet down, but as I peer through the gloom,
I just find fire-breakers, circuit-breakers and R numbers,
Social-distancing, lockdowns and Zoom.

We are teetering on the edge of a national lockdown,
One third of the country is now in tier three,
Locally, along with other areas, we've been placed on the 'watchlist',
That should mean more support and more tests, but we'll see.

It's now Saturday and the prime minister has made the announcement,
Lockdown is happening on Thursday, just four days to go,
Another month of solitary confinement,
Can I survive it? I really don't know.

Yes, I'm experienced, I know how to do it,
I developed strategies last time, which helped me get through,
But there's a weariness now where there was none,
I'm not sure that I know, how I'll do.

The disappointment is threatening to overwhelm me,
The frustration and resentment, as well,
Just when life was becoming more bearable,
I am returned to a mild form of hell.

I was managing quite well, I was coping,
I was back volunteering and going to art class,
I was having takeaways with friends wrapped in blankets,
We were tested but determined to pass.

Now, I'm faced with another uphill struggle,
When I'd just got used to a more level terrain,
I hope I can find that extra bit of energy,
Which I'll need to go through it again…

TWO HUNDRED AND THIRTY-FIVE DAYS

Still a little time left before Lockdown,
And you could say that I've had a bad day,
It started well, I went to art class, I was cheerful,
But I'm afraid it didn't finish that way.

I suppose it's that I really don't want to face it,
The fact that from next week, I will be on my own,
But reality struck when my friend said she couldn't meet me,
I was furious, doesn't she know that would mean I'm alone?

I don't know why I am taking this so personally,
There are plenty more in the same boat as me,
So much so that there's a new way to describe it,
It's called 'Alonement', a good word, you'll agree.

In normal circumstances, I would strongly recommend it,
Lots of personal space to breathe in and be free,
No one to consider, no one to annoy or upset you,
The silence is wonderful and I'm allowed to be me.

But of course, I still need lots of social interaction,
Usually I can choose when, with the options always there,
Whereas now, the Pandemic has curtailed the opportunities,
Making solitary living slightly more difficult to bear.

I am totally dependent now on planned 'get togethers',
Spontaneous contact is not available to me,
There's a touch issue as well, which is quite wounding,
No chance of random hugs or friendly gestures; do you see?...

TWO HUNDRED AND THIRTY-EIGHT DAYS

For a while now, I've been riding the Coronacoaster,
I didn't realise that I'd even got on,
It wasn't a conscious decision, I can assure you,
I never thought fairground rides were much fun.

But that's where I am and I don't know how it happened,
I'm strapped in now and I'm clinging to the side,
As I climb up and then drop down quite dramatically,
I was right, I do not like this kind of ride.

A few days ago, faced with yet another lockdown,
Deprived of company except for in the open air,
Totally out of control, I felt myself plunge headlong,
Into what could be, a kind of despair.

But then, the car I was in, slowly changed its position,
An upward motion, I leant back, more at ease,
I no longer felt I was being forced into a headwind,
Instead, it felt calmer with perhaps, just a light breeze.

Because I met friends at the South end of Walney,
We explored the nature reserve, there was plenty to do,
We met the warden, spied a rare egret and unusual herons,
Saw the lighthouse and the oyster farm too.

We ate our lunch sitting down on the pebbles,
Watching the birds give an aerial display,
The sea formed long horizontal waves which looked milky,
Reflecting the sky which was a silvery-grey.

The best part of the day was the seal-watching,
I was fascinated, just rooted to the spot,
They would break the surface, glide past, then slip under,
What a sight! One not easily forgot.

You see, the highs are very good, I just need them,
But I'm not sure where the Coronacoaster will go,
So, perhaps I'll get off at the next stop,
Could I do that? I really don't know…

TWO HUNDRED AND FORTY-FOUR DAYS

Yesterday was my daughter's big birthday,
Fifty years old she was, oh goodness me!
Of course, she had planned a very good party,
But Lockdown meant that it wasn't to be.

So, she had to be slightly inventive,
To make it an enjoyable day,
Friends and family all asked her for a time slot,
A good idea, she thought, we could do it that way.

It worked perfectly well for the most part,
Everything went smoothly, and according to plan,
Throughout the day, guests came with presents and good wishes,
Used the doorstep, and the big camper van.

Inside the house there was bunting and decorations,
There were balloons, lots of glitter and cake,
It really looked like there should be a party,
Virtual reality, let's make no mistake.

Still, as the surfaces filled up with presents,
I began to feel quite a warm glow,
She was loved, people had made an effort to please her,
I was a proud parent, I hoped it would show.

The day finished with some alcohol and a takeaway,
There was laughter and photo albums came out,
We looked back over the fifty years of her lifetime,
We'll celebrate it properly next year, there's no doubt.

TWO HUNDRED AND FORTY-SIX DAYS

I did a 'route-march' with my friend John, on Thursday,
It was a mistake to put him out in there in the lead,
I'd been celebrating birthdays, was hungover, slightly fragile,
Why didn't he realise I would prefer a slower speed?

But he was oblivious and he crashed on, quite determined,
To reach the far tip of Walney Island, was his aim,
We climbed up across, and down the sandhills, full of purpose,
Then slowly realised that they all looked just the same.

Still, after tramping through the mud, and brittle bracken,
After being stung by the sharp grasses, on each knee,
After tripping over hillocks and stumbling down crevasses,
We finally found the beach, and sat down, by the sea.

I ate the signature egg sandwich, surveyed the horizon,
And tried to identify the places in our view,
There were questions about the metal buildings and the turbines,
About the windsock and the Cellophane plant too.

After a while we set off back to find the car park,
John strode out decisively, trying to find a homeward route,
Despite a slight bit of contention and hesitation,
We decided it was best, perhaps, that we just follow suit.

Joking apart, I had loved nearly every minute,
The threatened storm had never happened, there was no rain,
We chatted freely, exchanging news and our opinions,
Can't wait 'til next week, when we'll do it all again.

TWO HUNDRED AND FORTY-EIGHT DAYS

This week, Covid and Brexit, are not first in the news headlines,
Instead, events in Number Ten have taken over that place,
There is a power struggle, conspiracy and tension,
Confrontation, a resignation and a fall from grace.

It started when the Director of Communications, was offered promotion,
He is a good friend of Dominic Cummings, you may know.
Unexpectedly, there were objections, which caused quite a backlash,
Under so much pressure, the offer was rescinded, he had to go.

It seems, along with Dominic, he'd been briefing against the Prime Minister,
They'd formed a faction and were critical, they both made it plain,
That they thought him indecisive, when they needed clarity,
Not really advisable, if you wish to remain.

Dominic was cross that his friend had been ousted,
Just when he was developing a solid power base; that was his aim,
But he hadn't reckoned on the challenge of two influential women,
With a similar objective and much better at that game.

Things came to a head in the Prime Minister's Cabinet office,
He was' livid' and he made it quite clear,
During a reportedly contentious and 'shouty' meeting,
That they must both leave at the end of the year.

There's a call now for a government reset,
A change in style is required, it's quite plain to see,
That a more harmonious approach would be much better,
Perhaps that is possible now, well maybe…

TWO HUNDRED AND FIFTY-ONE DAYS

What's going on? We're in November and there's sunshine,
It's been a glorious and a spring-like kind of day,
I spent it with friends, along the coast road, near the priory,
Another beach walk, but quite different, I must say.

We had to clamber over massive rocks and boulders,
It was a challenge, we had to find our own way through,
I teetered, precariously, quite often, on sharp edges,
Making bad decisions on where to land, I'm telling you!

It was an issue staying upright, but I made it,
I looked up, I breathed in deeply, admired the view,
The space seemed endless, and I let it totally absorb me,
I disappeared for a few moments; I just knew.

We walked on and found the cabin by the roadside,
We ordered lunch, and chose a bench right by the sea,
We let the watery sun attempt to warm us whilst we sat there,
No thoughts of lockdown and of guidelines, bothering me.

We wandered back through the woods, in a fug of warm confusion,
Underfoot there was some flooding, even bogs,
We negotiated tree roots, tangled wire, and abandoned bridges,
A playschool outing and a cemetery for dogs!

We were delighted when we ended up back where we started,
How did we do it? Well, I really do not know,
But what I do suspect is, that without the harsh restrictions,
We probably would not make the effort. We wouldn't go.

Our lockdown finishes on Wednesday, it's all over,
Then another ordeal begins, we're in tier two,
I don't listen to the news, I don't like the detail,
So, I'll have to Google what I can and cannot do.

It's a concern, because we're coming up to Christmas,
The new rules might have an impact, we will see,
But it's likely that there'll be some complications,
As my son in Manchester, is sadly, in tier three.

What?
It's a good job that I have a sense of humour,
"It would try the patience of a saint", (my mum would say),
I must admit, lately, that, my language is more colourful,
And I was near hysterical with my friend the other day.

We were sitting in the open air, as instructed,
Trying not to notice we were slowly turning blue,
It was early afternoon, but the sky was darkening,
The gloom enveloped us and took our brightness too.

I snuggled down into my blanket for some comfort,
I looked at my friend, who was sinking, I just knew,
Our eyes met, I said "How bl**** depressing is this?"
We laughed and laughed, what else was there to do?

Christmas is coming,
And I've been given a reprieve,
I can spend five days with my family,
Up to three households, I believe.

I've been counting on my fingers,
But the maths is not going well,
If I factor in the in-laws,
That's too many, I can tell.

Wait a minute, I'm in a bubble,
Does that mean just one, or is it two?
If I only knew the answer,
I'd be sure what I can do.

But, the more I think about it,
The more I think 'how cruel!',
And, the more I think it's likely,
That I'll bend this new-found rule...

All I didn't want for Christmas,
Was a new strain of Covid, that's for sure,
But that's what I got, and it's spreading quickly,
Just when we thought we had a cure.

The festive truce has now been cancelled,
We can't celebrate together, and what's more,
The Government has insisted on precautions,
There's a new tier now, tier four.

'If you've packed your bag, unpack it.'
That was the order of the day,
My son had bought his ticket, was getting ready,
Now he's not allowed to come and stay.

It's the same in other households,
Lots of people on their own,
I distinctly remember isolation,
I'm upset he'll be alone.

I don't like this Christmas present,
And, when all is said and done,
I think I'll write to Santa, and ask for,
A better 2021.

TWO HUNDRED AND NINETY DAYS

We're nearing the end of 2020,
Am I allowed a vestige of hope?
That my situation will get somewhat better,
And I'll find it much easier to cope.

The Pandemic has made life so difficult,
From my point of view, it's been tough,
But there are positives, which I have to consider,
There are a few, but, of course, not nearly enough.

It's made people become more kind-hearted,
Safe-guarding others and being more aware,
Of not spreading the dreaded infection,
By being considerate and showing more care.

It's made people be far more creative,
Expressing their feelings in all kinds of art,
Relearning skills that they'd put on the 'back-burner',
When they were busy and couldn't take part.

It's made people become much less selfish,
Sharing their groceries and supplying food banks,
Looking out for their elderly neighbours,
Doing it willingly and not just for thanks.

And, of course, it's been saving our planet,
Less travel meaning emissions are low,
The ozone layer is healing, the air is much fresher,
All good outcomes but yet even so…

2020 has been such a bad year,
Now, I know what I'm going to do,
I'll sit in the audience watching this pantomime,
And join in the chorus of, 'It's behind you!'.

Best place for it.

Sue Dower